THE ADVENTURES OF DIXIE
The Three-Legged Dog

Written by Connie Amarel
Illustrated by Swapan Debnath

This book is lovingly dedicated to Dixie, her family and friends (both human and animal), and in loving memory of Betty and Tom. It is also dedicated with love, admiration, blessings and best wishes to cancer survivors everywhere (both human and animal). Special thanks to my wonderful incredibly talented illustrator, Swapan.

This is the story of a truly remarkable three-legged dog named Dixie. A beautiful Lab/Shepherd mix, Dixie was born with four legs. When she was nine, her mom and dad (her owners) noticed she was limping.

They took her to see Dr. B, her veterinarian, who took an X-ray. It showed that she had cancer in her right front leg. The cancer was causing pain, which made her limp. Dr. B recommended surgery to remove her leg. The surgery would save Dixie's life by preventing the cancer from spreading and would make the pain go away.

Dr. B did such a great job that by the following morning Dixie was able to stand up. Although a little wobbly, she walked out in the yard to go potty. Dixie felt so much better not having pain anymore. Every day her left front leg became stronger and soon she was able to move as quickly as when she had four legs.

Dixie loved playing tug-of-war with her human brother and sister. Even with three legs Dixie tugged so hard on the rope they would have to let go. They laughed and fell on the ground because Dixie was so strong. She always licked their faces with "I got you" kisses while they hugged her tightly saying, "Good job, Dixie!"

Dr. B had a tall, handsome, German Wirehaired Pointer named Barney. He was so tall that Dixie could walk underneath him. Dixie and Barney became good friends. They would play at the park where Dixie ran as fast as any of the dogs who were playing there. Barney was very protective of Dixie and ran beside her at the park.

Dixie had another friend named Neige. He was an enormous, handsome, and lovable Black Lab whose nickname was Moose. He would play with Dixie at her house. Barney and Moose came to Dixie's birthday parties and the three friends had so much fun chasing each other around the yard. Dixie loved her friends and was always happy to see them.

One day Dixie was playing in the back yard when she suddenly started barking very loudly. She ran into the house, pacing back and forth between her mom and dad and the sliding glass door. Dixie's mom and dad knew that something must be wrong and that she wanted them to follow her. They quickly got up and ran outside.

Dixie was standing by the fence that separated her yard from the neighbor's yard. Her dad looked over the fence and saw a puppy in the swimming pool trying to climb out, but every time falling back into the pool.

Dixie's dad ran to the neighbor's back yard and gently lifted the puppy out of the pool. The puppy was wet and very tired, but wagged its tail. It was so happy to be out of the pool. Dixie saved the puppy's life.

Dixie was so happy when her mom and dad's friends, Tom and Betty, came to visit. Dixie loved Betty and tried to get as close to her as possible. Tom and Betty always sat on the loveseat together. When Tom got up, Dixie jumped on the loveseat where he had been sitting. She wanted to sit next to Betty.

When Tom came back, Dixie wouldn't move to let him sit down. Tom laughed and said, "Hey, that's my gal you're sitting next to!" But Dixie wouldn't budge. She wanted Betty all to herself. Betty thought it was so funny that Dixie wouldn't let Tom have his seat back.

Dixie always got excited when the UPS truck pulled up in front of the house. She loved barking at the UPS man. He would say "Hi!" to her through the door when he put a package on the front porch.

One day he dropped off a package and Dixie's mom opened the door right away to pick it up. Before she could close the door, Dixie ran out, chasing the laughing UPS man back to his truck. She then ran back and forth in front of the truck, barking loudly and wagging her tail. Dixie was determined to defend the neighborhood from the UPS truck.

The UPS man smiled because he thought it was great that a dog with three legs could be so fierce and fearless. Dixie's mom called her back to the house and gave her a special treat for protecting the neighborhood.

Dixie loved going for walks. When children walked by, they would ask why Dixie had only three legs. Dixie's mom and dad would explain that she had cancer in her leg and it was removed to save her life. The children always wanted to pet Dixie and she really enjoyed the extra attention.

One sunny afternoon Dixie and her mom took a walk around the block. They passed by a gardener who was bending over putting yard clippings into a trash bag. Dixie nudged the gardener's behind making him fall forward.

He quickly looked back to see who had nudged him. Dixie had moved on leaving her mom standing behind him, so the gardener thought Dixie's mom nudged him. She started to explain that it was Dixie who nudged him, but Dixie tugged on the leash making her mom move down the sidewalk without being able to explain.

When Dixie's mom told her dad what had happened, they both laughed so hard. Dixie was very smart and knew just what she was doing. Dixie smiled and wagged her tail. She thought it was funny, too.

Dixie's mom had a friend who came to visit with her toddler. This toddler loved Danish butter cookies, and so did Dixie. The toddler's mom handed him a cookie and then turned around to talk to Dixie's mom.

Dixie saw the cookie in the toddler's hand, licked her lips and then gently but quickly snatched it from his hand. The toddler started to cry because he wanted a cookie and didn't get one.

His mom handed him another cookie and turned around to talk. Dixie gently snatched the cookie and he cried again. This went on several more times until the toddler's mom, who had been so busy talking with Dixie's mom, suddenly realized that he was eating way too many cookies.

She gave him another cookie but said it was going to be the last one. This time she didn't turn around to talk and saw Dixie gently snatch the cookie from her toddler's hand. Now she knew why he wanted so many cookies and why Dixie was always nearby, smiling and wagging her tail.

There are many reasons why Dixie is a truly remarkable three-legged dog. But the most important reason is the valuable lesson she has taught her family, friends, and everyone lucky enough to meet her.

Sometimes bad things, like cancer, may happen. If we stand up to those bad things the same fearless way that Dixie stood up to the UPS truck, allow ourselves to laugh, eat lots of cookies, and maybe even wag our tails, life can be a wonderful adventure!

15107651R00019